LOCOMOTIVES & CC
OF TH
NETHERLANDS RAILWAYS

The complete guide to all NS Locomotives
and Passenger Rolling Stock

Gordon Lacy & Peter Fox

PLATFORM
5

Published by Platform 5 Publishing Ltd., 15 Abbeydale Park Rise, Sheffield S17 3PB.
Printed by Heanor Gate Printing Ltd., Delves Road, Heanor Gate Industrial Estate,
Heanor, Derbyshire.
ISBN 0 906579 38 4
© 1984 Platform 5 Publishing Ltd.

INTRODUCTION

This book contains full details of all locomotives, multiple units and coaching stock of the Netherlands Railways. In Dutch this is Nederlandse Spoorwegen, hereafter abreviated to NS. Information is updated to 1st January 1984.
The NS is a relatively small system and approximately two thirds of all routes are electrified at 1500 Vdc with overhead wire collection. The NS have a large number of emus which formerly worked most internal passenger trains, but recently a number of routes have changed to locomotive-haulage with the introduction of the Plan ICR Inter City coaches.
The NS timetable is almost entirely regular interval with most routes having half-hourly services and many routes four trains per hour.
Language presents no problem, since most dutch people speak good english, but restaurant menus are often in dutch only, so a dictionary or phrase book can still be useful.

Railway enthusiasts will find the NS 3 and 7-day rover tickets very useful. At the time of writing these cost £18.50 2nd class and £27.50 1st class for the three-day card and £25 2nd class and £37 1st class for the seven day card.

The principal services on the NS are to be found in the first section of their public timetable (Tables A-H). These are outlined below giving the motive power details for the services as a guide for those interested in travelling on the different types of locomotive and multiple unit to be found on NS. See also the map on the back cover.

Route A. Amsterdam/Haarlem-Alkmaar-Den Helder/Hoorn.
All services are emus, usually in the 4xx, 8xx and 9xx series.

Route B. Amsterdam-Haarlem-Den Haag-Rotterdam-Dordrecht-Roosendaal-Vlissingen /Brussels.
Amsterdam — Brussels services are either push-pull trains with SNCB dual-current Electric locos (2551-2558 series), or 12xx (& SNCB 220901 series) dual current emus, Amsterdam — Vlissingen services are mainly hauled trains with 1100, 1200 or 1600 class electric locos, certain off peak services being 7xx or 17xx EMUs.

Route C. Hoek van Holland/Den Haag-Rotterdam-Dordrecht-Tilburg-Eindhoven-venlo-(Köln).
Hoek van Holland/Den Haag-Venlo (Köln) services are loco hauled with 1500 and 1600 class electrics. Some turns are 1100 or 1200 hauled and certain weekend services have 1300 haulage. The Köln through services are usually worked forward from Venlo by DB 110 series electrics.

Route D. Zandvoort-Haarlem-Amsterdam-Utrecht-Den Bosch-Eindhoven-Sittard-Maastricht/Heerlen.
Zandvoort-Maastricht/Heerlen services are normally loco hauled and are shared between 1200 and 1600 electrics with some trains having 1100 or 1300 haulage.

Route E. Amsterdam/Den Haag/Rotterdam-Utrecht-Arnhem/Nijmegen -Köln/Hagen.
Den Haag/Rotterdam-Arnhem services are emu turns as are some Amsterdam-Arnhem trains, 40xx IC 3 emus work the Amsterdam-Arnhem/Nijmegen services in pairs. Amsterdam-Köln/Hagen and some Arnhem services are worked by 1100, 1300 and 1600 electrics with some 1200 turns. The Köln/Hagen services are worked forward from Emmerich by DB 110 series Electrics. The Köln via Nijmegen services are worked forward from Arnhem with DB 215, 216 or 218 series diesel hydraulics.

Route F. Zwolle-Deventer-Arnhem-Nijmegen-Den Bosch-Tilburg-Roosendaal/ Vlissingen.
Zwolle-Roosendaal/Vlissingen services are usually 1100 or 1200 hauled although 1600 and 1300 at weekends, also make an appearance.

Route G. Amsterdam-Amersfoort/Den Haag -Rotterdam-Utrecht-Amersfoort-Deventer Hengelo (-Hannover)-Enschede.
Den Haag/Rotterdam-Enschede services are emu turns. All Amsterdam — Hannover via Bad Bentheim, and most Enschede services are loco hauled by 1100, 1200 and 1300 and occasional 1600 turns. Hannover services are usually worked forward from Bad Bentheim by DB 110 series Electrics.

Route H. Amsterdam-Amersfoort / Den Haag-Rotterdam-Utrecht -Amersfoort-Zwolle-Leeuwarden/Groningen.
Amsterdam, Den Haag/Rotterdam-Leeuwarden/Groningen services are all emu turns with 3xx, 7xx and 17xx series units.

CLASS DIMENSIONS

Principal dimensions are given for each class in metric units. Imperial equivalents are also given except for weight, as the difference is small between a metric tonne and the imperial ton (1 ton = 1.016 tonnes). Standard abbreviations used in this book are:

hp	horse power	lbf	pounds force
km/h	kilometres per hour	mph	miles per hour
kN	kilonewtons	t	tonnes
kW	kilowatts		

VEHICLE TYPE CODES FOR MULTIPLE-UNITS AND HAULED STOCK

These are given in the Dutch system with the English codes in parentheses.

(1) DUTCH SYSTEM:
f—   Bicycle van (Dutch —bicycles = fietsen)
k—   Driving Cab
m—   Motor (with driving cab(s))
r—   Restaurant
s—   Driving Trailer
A—   1st Class
B—   2nd Class
D—   Luggage, i.e., vehicle with luggage space and guard's compartment
K—   Buffet Kitchen
P—   Post, ie, vehicle with compartment/s for mail (and guard)
Examples:
BDk — Driving Second Class with luggage/guard's compartment.
AB — Composite.
Note — NS do not differentiate between open and compartment stock or indicate toilet facilities in their coding system.

(2) BRITISH SYSTEM
Coaching stock codes are as used in Multiple Unit Pocket Book and Coaching Stock Pocket Book, e.g., F=first, S=second, C=composite, B=brake, O=open, K=side corridor with lavatory, so=semi-open.
The number of seats, lavatory compartments and washrooms are shown as nF nS nL nW, eg: 80S 2L 2W has 80 second class seats, two lavatory compartments and two washrooms.

NUMBERING

Whilst locos and emus have simple two, three or four digit numbers, the loco-hauled coaching stock is numbered according to the UIC twelve digit scheme. This is explained on page 34.

KEEPING THIS BOOK UP TO DATE

Readers can keep this book up to date by becoming members of the Locomotive Club of Great Britain, whose bulletin, supplied to all members, contains details of stock changes for many continental railways. For details of membership send a stamped self-addressed envelope to Hon. General Secretary, 8 Lovatt Close, Edgware, Middlesex, HA8 9XG.

Plan A (1946 stock) 4-car emu no. 687 at Vlissingen. All of these green liveried emus nicknamed "cucumbers" are now withdrawn from capital stock. The following 2-car units survive however:
231   Departmental service
273   Preserved by "STIBANS"
279   Departmental service
285   Departmental test car (now 80 84 978-2 504-8
291   Departmental instruction car (now 30 84 978-2 503-1)

FRONT COVER PHOTOGRAPH: 1500 class Co-Co no 1505, formerly British Railways class EM2 no 27001 ARIADNE at Den Haag Centraal Station with the 19.57 to Köln. The first coach is an SNCF "Corail" vehicle.   [Ian Gould

4

DIESEL-ELECTRIC SHUNTING LOCOS

200 CLASS   0-4-0

These small, but useful, locomotives, known as "Sik", can be seen virtually all over the NS system at work on light duties or in yards where the more powerful 500/600 Class are not required. Large concentrations can be found in the Dock areas of Amsterdam and Rotterdam as well as the situations mentioned under the 500/600 Class (qv.). Small permanent-way trains can often be noted with a 200 in charge, often one fitted with a telescopic crane. Also of interest is the sight of these locos being driven from the outside, controls on the cabsides being used. They have been built over quite a lengthy period, from 1934 to 1951, later locomotives being replacements for war losses. Some have been sold out of stock for private use. Most of the locos have now been repainted from dark green to the current yellow/grey livery, the number plates being removed at the same time in common with other NS locomotives.

Built: 1934-51 by Werkspoor (281-306 by N.S., Zwolle Works)
Engine: Stork R153 of 63 kW (85 hp)
Traction motors: Two Heemaf TM6 or Smit GT322/7 axle hung.
Tractive effort: 39 kN (8800 lbf) max, 12 kN (2650 lbf) continuous at 12 mph.
Weight: 21 t (23 t*).
Length: 7.22 m (23' 7½").
Wheel dia: 1000 mm (3'3⅜")
Max. speed: 60 km/h (37 mph)
*Fitted with telescopic crane

203	243	279	312	339
204	244	281	313	340
209	245	283	314	341
210	246*	284	315	342
211	247	285	316	343
213	248*	286	318	344
214	249	288	319	345
215	250*	289	320	346
217	252	290	321	347
218	253	291	322	348
219	254	292	323	349
222	255	296	324	350
223	256	297	325	351
225	257	298	326	352
226	259	299	327	353
227*	260	300	328	355*
228	262	301	329	357
229	263	302	330	358
230	264	303	331	359
231	265*	305	332	360*
232	267	306	334	361*
234	270	307	335	362*
235	271	308	336	363
238	274*	309*	337	368*
241	276*	310	338	369
242*	278			

200 Class shunter with telescopic crane no. 355 at Amsterdam C.S. on 25th March 1982.   [Gordon Lacy

500/600 class E.E. Shunters nos 536 and 602 at Tilburg Works.   [Mike Jacob

6

550/600 CLASSES   0-6-0

These locomotives represent the most recognisable link with the British system being vitually identical, apart from train air-braking, with the former Class 11 and the Class 08 Shunters of British Rail. They also perform similar work, i.e., shunting in marshalling yards, principal goods yards and station pilots. Although fairly widespread in distribution, reasonable numbers can be found in the Docks at Amsterdam and Rotterdam, Amsterdam Carriage Sidings, Amsterdam Yards (between Muiderport and Dieren stations), Kijfhoek Yards (between Barendrecht and Zwijndrecht stations), Maastricht and Amersfoort Yards. Smaller numbers are to be found at Venlo, Eindhoven, Zwolle, Utrecht, Hengelo and other principal stations. Tilburg Works sees a continuous throughput of the class and several are normally to be seen in the works yard alongside Tilburg station. At least one (517) survives in private use. All now carry the NS POP livery.

Built: 1950-57 by English Electric (Dick Kerr Works, Preston).
Engine: English Electric 6 K of 260 kW (350 hp) (500 class) 6KT of 294 kW (400 hp) (600 class).
Traction motors: Two EE 506 axle-hung.
Tractive effort: 143 kN (32100 lbf), max., 64 kN (14435 lbf) continuous at 10 mph.
Weight: 47t
Length: 9.07 m (29'9").
Wheel dia: 1230 mm (4'0⅜").
Max speed: 30 km/h (18.5 mph).
*Fitted with radio.

512	542	615	632	649
521	543	616	633	650
523	544	617	634	651
524	545	618	635	652
525	601	619	636	653
526	602	620	637	654
528	603	621	638	655
529	604	622	639	656
530	605	623	640	657
531	606	624	641	658
532	607	625	642	659
533	608	626*	643	660
534	609*	627	644	661
536	610	628	645	662
537	611	629	646	663
538	612	630	647	664
540	613	631	648	665
541	614			

ELECTRIC LOCOMOTIVES
1100 CLASS   Bo-Bo

The Alsthom-built 1100 Class are based on the French (SNCF) class BB-8100 which date from 1949. These are basically freight locomotives with a maximum speed of 65 mph (105 km/h). By fitting spring-borne traction motors the maximum speed on the NS1100 is raised to 84 mph (135 km/h) giving a useful mixed-traffic locomotive. Early locomotives (1101-50) were delivered in light blue livery, this being soon altered to the dark blue introduced in 1954 and enhanced with raised polished metal bands. Apart from the addition of the modern NS "logo", this remained standard until 1971 when a

1100 class no. 1118 (in old blue livery) at Den Haag H.S. on 7th October 1982.
[Peter Fox

1200 class no. 1207 approaches Amersfoort with train of DB stock. [Mike Jacob

1117,18 & 38 having full yellow noses as on the POP-liveried version. These locos have recently been altered to yellow panels only as on other blue examples. Other alterations have consisted of the fitting of roller bearings to overcome lively riding and larger, sleeve type buffers similar to those on the new 1600 Class.

Built: 1950-6 by Alsthom (Rebuilt by NS 1978-82).
Continuous rating: 1925 kW (2580 hp)
Max. tractive effort: 152 kN (34200 lbf)
Continuous tractive effort: 64 kN (14300 lbf) at 50 km/h
Length: 14.11 m (46'3¾").
Max. speed: 135 km/h (84 mph).
Weight: 83t.
Wheel dia: 1250 mm (4' 1¼")
b— Still in blue livery at time of writing.

1101	1113	1125	1138 b	1149
1102	1114 b	1126	1139	1150
1103 b	1115 b	1127	1140	1151
1104	1116 b	1128	1141	1152
1105 b	1117 b	1129	1142	1153
1106 b	1118 b	1130	1143	1154
1107	1119	1132	1144	1155
1108 b	1120	1133 b	1145	1157
1109	1121 b	1134	1146	1158
1110 b	1122	1135 b	1147	1159
1111	1123	1136	1148	1160
1112	1124	1137		

1200 CLASS   Co-Co

The striking 1200 Class, originally built for freight haulage, were constructed as "kit-form" locomotives, with the bogies being supplied by Baldwin and electrical components from Westinghouse, the classic "American" styling clearly showing their design origin. Werkspoor of Amsterdam constructed the bodies, remaining electrical gear being supplied by Heemaf. The mixed parentage of the locos was, until recently, displayed on the characteristic workplates carried on the nose-ends. As the locomotives are re-furbished, these are removed, other visible differences being in the arrangement of lights on the nose-ends. Although originally designed for 93 mph (150 km/h) capability, these are restricted to 84 mph (135 km/h) on NS lines. Extremely popular with their NS crews, all locos are in the standard grey and yellow livery.

Built: 1951-3 (Rebuilt 1978-83)
Traction motors: Six Heemaf TM94 axle-hung.
Continuous rating: 2240 kW (3000 hp).
Max. speed: 135 km/h (84 mph).
Max. tractive effort: 193 kN (43500 lbf).
Continuous tractive effort: 99 kN (22400 lbf) at 50 km/h.
Weight: 108t.
Length: 18.08 m (59'4").
Wheel dia: 1100 mm (3'7⅜").

1201	1206	1211	1216	1221
1202	1207	1212	1217	1222
1203	1208	1213	1218	1223
1204	1209	1214	1219	1224
1205	1210	1215	1220	1225

1300 class no. 1314 at Arnhem on 25th March 1983 with the 17.17 Amsterdam C.S.—Köln (DB stock). [Gordon Lacy

1500 class no. 1503 (formerly B.R. no. 27004 JUNO) waits to leave Den Haag C.S. with the 15.45 to Siegen on 22nd January 1984. [Ian Gould

1300 CLASS   Co-Co

The impressive looking 1300 Class are based on the SNCF Alsthom-built CC-7100 Class which includes in its ranks CC-7107, the co-world record speed holder (205.6 mph attained in 1955). The NS 1300 duties are much less glamorous, being generally utilised for heavy freight work with only limited passenger diagrams, principally at weekends. One example, 1313, carries the more modern "elbow" type pantographs instead of the standard "box" type. Most of the class carry the POP livery, the only variation being that some have yellow cab-side handrails, others grey. The last two in the older, dark blue livery at the time of writing (1307,10) differ slightly from one another in that 1307 does not retain the bright metal trim on the cab doors.

Built: 1952-6.
Traction motors: Six Alsthom TA 628 A frame mounted.
Continuous rating: 2890 kW (3870 hp).
Max. speed: 135 km/h (84 mph).
Max tractive effort: 227 kN (51000 lbf).
Continuous tractive effort: 127 kN (28600 lbf) at 50 km/h.
Length: 18.95 m (62'2")
Weight: 111t.
Wheel dia: 1250 mm (4'1¼").

1301	1305	1308	1311	1314
1302	1306	1309	1312	1315
1304	1307 b	1310 b	1313	1316

1500 CLASS (BR CLASS EM2)   Co-Co

These familiar locomotives have probably been the reason that many British enthusiasts have visited the Dutch system for the first time. Extensively re-built after purchase from British Rail by the NS, they are still much in evidence on passenger and freight work over the Den Haag to Venlo route and are often to be seen at Hoek van Holland, an appropriate welcome to British visitors. Obvious external differences, apart from the POP livery, since entering service in 1970, have been the replacement of the "box" pantographs, re-modelling of the cab fronts, changeover to right-hand drive, air-braking, removal of boiler water tanks and replacement with air cylinders. A more recent alteration consists of removal of the distinctive oval buffers and replacement with the larger rectangular "sleeve" style as on the 1100 Class.

Built 1954. Formerly worked on the Manchester-Sheffield line (via Woodhead).
Traction motors: Six Metropolitan-Vickers MV 146 Axle-hung.
Continuous rating: 1932 kW (2590 hp).
Max speed: 135 km/h. Note–this is the NS maximum. On BR they were limited to 90 mph.
Max tractive effort: 200 kN (45000 lbf).
Continuous tractive effort: 91 kN (20000 lbf) at 78 km/h.
Length: 18.10 m (59'4⅝").
Weight 98t.
Wheel dia: 1092 mm (3'7").

NS	BR	NS	BR
1501	(27003 DIANA)	1504	(27006 PANDORA)
1502	(27000 ELECTRA)	1505	(27001 ARIADNE)
1503	(27004 JUNO)	1506	(27002 AURORA)

1600 CLASS   B-B

Currently being named after towns on the NS electric lines, the thyristor controlled 1600 class represents a major investment programme in Dutch railways. The bright yellow locomotives are based on the SNCF Alsthom BB-15000 Class designed for maximum speeds of 125 mph (although limited at present to 100 mph). The NS locos perform mixed traffic duties over all the principal routes. It is proposed to utilise 1600 locos on push-pull double-deck outer suburban trains to the North of Amsterdam, the original order of 48 being extended to 58 to cater for this eventuality. The livery first applied to 1601-15 had the large number centrally positioned but later locos were delivered with numbers at the left hand side to make room for the transfer-applied names on the right-hand end. The earlier locos are being altered to conform as names are applied.

Built: 1981-3 by Alsthom.
Traction motors: Two Alsthom TAB 674 C4, frame mounted.
Continuous rating: 4400 kW (5900 hp).
Max speed:160 km/h (100 mph).
Max tractive effort: 294 kN (66100 lbf).
Continuous tractive effort: 135 kN (30400 lbf) at 106.5 km/h.
Weight: 83t.
Length: 17.48 m (57'4⅛'').
Wheel dia: 1250 mm (4'1¼'').

1601	Amsterdam	1630	
1602		1631	Voorburg
1603		1632	Nijmegen
1604	Dordrecht	1633	Bergen op Zoom
1605	Breda	1634	
1606		1635	Enschede
1607	Vlissingen	1636	
1608		1637	Amersfoort
1609		1638	
1610	Hengelo	1639	Leiden
1611	Venlo	1640	
1612	Goes	1641	
1613	Roermond	1642	
1614		1643	
1615	Zandvoort	1644	Roosendaal
1616		1645	Middelburg
1617		1646	
1618	Almelo	1647	
1619	Maastricht	1648	
1620	Arnhem	1649	Oss
1621	Deventer	1650	
1622	Haarlem	1651	Tilburg
1623	Hilversum	1652	
1624		1653	Den Helder
1625		1654	Geleen
1626	Meppel	1655	Eindhoven
1627	Gouda	1656	Hoogeveen
1628	Apeldoorn	1657	Rotterdam
1629		1658	Zaandam

MAIN-LINE DIESEL-ELECTRICS LOCOS
2200 CLASS
Bo-Bo

The similarity with the British Class 20 extends to the kind of duties which these locos are called upon to perform. Double-heading, or singly, the principal work is freight and they are to be found all over the NS system. Some of the class working in the marshalling yards at Kijfhoek, near Rotterdam are radio-fitted for ease of communication with the control-towers. They may also be found on station pilot work especially at Amsterdam Centraal where re-marshalling of some of the long distance trains takes place. Just as in Britain, these "Type 1's" have a limited passenger usage, although the regular working on the Arnhem to Winterswijk line has now been discontinued.
This was especially interesting as it was a push-pull turn with a train-heating vehicle marshalled at the rear of the passenger stock which is stencilled "DE" to indicate suitability for diesel haulage. The vast majority of the locos are now in the POP livery which has superseded the former reddish-brown previously carried and which was augmented, as were the electric locos, with large, ornate numberplates on the ends with oval plates on the sides. Certain locos are in the process of being fitted with large central headlights, which with the "marker" lights give the familiar triangle of lights to be found on the Continent and now on the class 56 locos of B.R.

Built: 1955-58 by Allan (2201-2300), Schneider (2301-50).
Engine: Stork Schneider Superior 40C-Lx-8 of 671 kW (900 hp) at 1100 rpm.
Traction motors: Four Heemaf TM98 188 kW (250 hp) axle-hung.
Max. tractive effort: 181 kN (40800 lbf)
Continuous tractive effort: 120 kN (27000 lbf) at 14 km/h.
Wheel dia: 950 mm (3'1⅜").　　　　　　*Weight: 72t.*
Max. speed: 100 km/h (62 mph).　　　*Length: 14.10 m (45'11½").*
*-radio fitted　　h-headlight fitted　　r-red/brown livery at time of writing.

2201	2229	2257	2285	2317
2202	2230	2258 r	2286	2218 r
2203	2232 (ex2222)	2259	2288 r	2319 r
2204	2233 (ex2208)	2260*	2289	2320
2205 (ex2226)	2234	2261*r	2290	2322
2206	2235 h	2263*r	2291 h	2323
2207	2236 (ex2221)	2264*	2292	2324
2208 (ex2233)	2237 (ex2210)	2265*	2293	2326 r
2209	2238	2266*	2294 h	2327
2210 r (ex2237)	2239	2267*	2295	2328
2211	2240	2268*	2296	2329
2212	2241	2269* (ex2218)	2297	2330
2213	2242	2270*	2298	2332
2214	2243 h	2271	2299	2333
2215	2244 h	2272	2300	2334
2216	2245 h	2273	2301	2335
2217	2246	2274 r	2302 r	2336
2219 (ex2231)	2247 r	2275 r	2303	2338
2220	2249	2276 r	2304	2339
2221 (ex2236)	2250 h	2277 r	2305	2340
2222 (ex2232)	2251 h	2278 r	2306	2342
2223 (ex2278)	2252 r	2280	2307	2343
2224 (ex2227)	2253	2281 r	2308	2344
2225	2254	2282	2309 r	2345
2226 (ex2205)	2255	2283 r	2310 r	2346
2227 (ex2224)	2256 h	2284 r	2311	2348
2228 h (ex2223)				

2200 class DE no. 2215 at Tilburg Works.   [Mike Jacob

The unique no. 2530 at Dordrecht in March 1982.   [Peter Heppenstall

14

2400 CLASS   Bo-Bo

These locomotives, with a resemblance to the former B.T.H. locos of B.R., also perform freight duties over the whole of the NS system. However they do not perform on passenger trains except in the unusual case of a failure of an electric where no other loco is available. One significant turn which is of interest is on the quadruple-headed ore trains which make a stirring sight and sound lumbering through Eindhoven. Livery details are the same as the 2200 Class, with which they are sometimes found in multiple.

Built: 1954-56 by Alsthom.
Engine: SACM V12 SHR of 626 kW (850 hp).
Traction motors: Four Alsthom TA 637 150 kW (200 hp) axle-hung.
Max. tractive effort: 161 kN (36400 lbf).
Continuous tractive effort: (12830 lbf) at 20 km/h.
Weight: 60t.
Length: 12.52 m (41'1").
Wheel dia: 1000 mm (3'3⅜").
Max speed: 80 km/h (50 mph).
h-headlight fitted   r-red/brown livery at time of writing

2401	2424 h	2449	2477	2504
2402	2425	2450	2478	2505 r
2403	2426	2451	2479	2506
2404	2428 h	2452	2480	2508
2405	2429	2453	2481	2509
2406	2430 h	2454	2482	2510
2407	2431 h	2456 r	2483	2511
2408	2432 h	2457	2484	2512
2409	2433	2458	2486	2513
2410	2434	2459	2487	2514 r
2411	2435	2461	2488 r	2515
2412	2436	2462	2489	2516
2413	2437	2463	2490 r	2518
2414	2439	2465	2491	2520
2415 h	2440	2466	2492	2522
2416 h	2441	2467	2493	2524
2417 r	2442	2469	2495	2525
2418	2443	2470	2498	2526
2419 h	2444	2471	2500	2527
2420 h	2446	2472 r	2501 r	2528
2422	2447	2474	2502	2529
2423	2448	2475	2503	

2530 CLASS   Bo-Bo

The sole representative of its type, this locomotive works the same duties as the 2400 Class of which it is basically a modification. It is, however, most unusual in carrying small "cabins" on opposite corners making it a most distinctive locomotive. It carries the new POP livery.

Details as for 2400 Class except length which is 13.30 m (43'7⅝").
2530

Plan X (DEII) articulated two-car unit at Zwolle on 1st July 1983. [Peter Heppenstall

Plan U (DEIII) three car diesel electric unit no. 120 at Enschede on 23rd March 1982. **[Gordon Lacy**

DIESEL-ELECTRIC MULTIPLE UNITS

V.I.P. CAR
"THE CAMEL"

This ex-directors saloon nicknamed "The Camel" is available for party hire and may be
:seen virtually anywhere. The yellow livery is enhanced by a blue stripe, and the raised
:driving positions and lack of auto-coupling make this a very distinctive unit.

Built: 1954 by Allan
Engine: AEC A220 of 134 kW (180 hp)
Seats: 24F 2L

Weight: 58 t
Length: 25.55 m (83'9⅞")
Max speed: 125 km/h (78 mph)

20

PLAN X (CLASS DEI)
SINGLE UNITS

The survivors of this red-liveried class have latterly worked services such as Almelo-
Marienberg, Zwolle-Kampen, Heerlen-Valkenberg and Maastricht-Liege. This class is
disappearing rapidly.

Built: 1953-5 by Allan
Engine: AEC A220 of 209 kW (280 hp)
Formation: ABD or BD (DMBCOL or DMBSOL)
Max speed: 120km/h (75 mph)

Weight: 57 t
Length: 2705 m (88'9")
Seats: 8F 65S 1L or 73S 1L

21	25	34	36	41
22	33			

PLAN X (CLASS DEII) SIX AXLE ARTICULATED UNITS

Also in the older red livery, the remaining un-converted units work such turns as
Zwolle-Kampen, Arnhem/Nijmegen-Teil and Apeldoorn-Winterswijk. They have recently
been displaced from the branch lines to the north of Groningen by the new 3201 series
units. Numbers are diminishing due to conversion or withdrawal.

Built: 1953-4 by Allan
Engine: Two AEC A220 of 170 kW (240 hp)
Formation:BDk—ABk (DMBSOL-DMCOL)
Max. speed: 120 km/h (75 mph)

Weight: 86 t
Length: 45.4 m
Seats: 60S 1L + 28F 45S 1L (or 73S 1L)

71	77	81	93	96
74	78	85	95	101
76	80			

PLAN U (CLASS DEIII)
3-CAR UNITS

In many respects similar in appearance to the 1962 stock emus, these three-car "dog
head" demus work over the following lines: Dordrecht-Geldermalsen, Roermond-
Nijmegen, Zwolle-Enschede and Emmen, Arnhem-Winterswijk. Fitted with automatic
doors and pa.

Built: 1960-3 by Werkspoor
Engine: RUHB 1616 of 746 kW (1000 hp) or MGO 12*
Formation: mBDk—B—ABk (DMBSO-TSOL-DTCsoL)
Max speed: 125 km/h (78 mph)

Weight: 136 t
Length: 73.73 m (241'11")
Seats: 40S + 88S 2L + 24F 40S 2L

111	115	119	123	127
112*	116	120	124	128*
113*	117	121	125	129
114*	118*	122*	126	130

131*	136	141	145*	149
132	137	142	146	150*
133*	138	143*	147	151*
134	139*	144	148	152*
135*	140			

PLAN X-v (Rebuilt CLASS DEII)
6-AXLE ARTICULATED UNITS

These units (ex 61-106 series) have been extensively rebuilt and modernised and are easily distinguishable from the original sets by the application of the standard yellow livery. They work on similar turns, ie, Arnhem/Nijmegen-Teil, and also on Arnhem-Doetinchem, Apeldoorn-Winterswijk, Enschede-Zutphen as well as in the north on the branches from Leeuwarden.

Rebuilt: 1975, 1977-82 at NS Haarlem workshops
Engines: Two Cummins 180 kW (240 hp)   *Weight: 86 t*
Formation: ABk—Bk (DMCOL-DMSOL)   *Length: 45.4 m (148'7¾")*
Seats: 16F 56S 1L + 76S 1L
Original numbers are shown in parentheses.

161 (88)	167 (61)	172 (66)	177 (62)	182 (75)
162 (92)	168 (91)	173 (100)	178 (82)	183 (67)
163 (83)	169 (94)	174 (70)	179 (72)	184 (65)
164 (106)	170 (69)	175 (68)	180 (73)	185 (102)
165 (103)	171 (98)	176 (64)	181 (99)	186 (87)
166 (97)				

ELECTRIC MULTIPLE UNITS

All NS emus are gangwayed within the unit only and have tread brakes except where stated otherwise.

The various builds of NS emu can easily be recognised by their front-end design as follows:

1946 stock had a round front and in addition had a characteristic green livery. All 1946 stock is now withdrawn, but some may be seen in sidings awaiting scrapping.
1954 stock has a large "dog nose" and was designed for Inter-City services.
1964 stock has a single shorter "dog nose" with the outer cab windows pointed. It is used on stopping services.
"Sprinter" stock has a slightly sloping front end.
IC-III stock has a gangwayed end with a roof cab.
EMUs are often referred to by their formation codes as follows:
EL=emu   D=includes guard/luggage area (dienst)   2,3 or 4=no. of cars.
Example: ELD-2 — Two car emu with guard/luggage accommodation.

PLAN F,G,M&Q   TWO-CAR UNITS

These sets are used on local routes such as Utrecht C.S.-Teil and Rhenen and Amsterdam C.S.-Arnhem, and to strengthen 711 series workings (q.v.). Fitted with automatic doors and PA.

Built: 1956-8 by Allan (F,G,M) 1962 by Werkspoor (Q). "1954 Stock"
Formation: ABDK–Bk (DMBCOL–DMSsoL)   *Seats: 24F 24S 1L+72S 1L*
Traction motors: Four Smit Heemaf 169kW (227 hp)   *Weight: 110t (104 t Plan Q)*
Max speed: 140 km/h (87 mph)   *Length 51.12 m (167'4½")*
321-334 are Plan F, 335-350 are Plan G, 351-365 are Plan M and 371-393 are Plan Q.

321	335	349	362	381
322	336	350	363	382
323	337	351	364	383
324	338	352	365	384
325	339	353	371	385
326	340	354	372	386
327	341	355	373	387
328	342	356	374	388
329	343	357	375	389
330	344	358	376	390
331	345	359	377	391
332	346	360	378	392
333	347	361	379	393
334	348			

PLAN V   2-CAR UNITS

These sets perform similar duties to the 321 series on local stopping trains on routes such as Amsterdam C.S.-Arnhem, Rotterdam C.S.-Nijmegen, Utrecht C.S.-Leiden.

Built: 1966-8 by Werkspoor. "1962 stock", Automatic doors. PA
Formation: ABDk-Bk (DMBCOL–DMSsoL)
Traction motors: Four Smit 188 kW (252 hp)   *Seats: 24F 24S 1L +80S 1L*
Weight: 85 t   *Length: 52.14 m (170'3")*
Max. speed: 140 km/h (87 mph)

401	409	417	425	432
402	410	418	426	433
403	411	419	427	434
404	412	421	428	435
405	413	422	429	436
406	414	423	430	437
407	415	424	431	438
408	416			

PLAN V   2-CAR UNITS

These units are similar to 401-438 but have no luggage compartment. They work very short-distance traffic such as Amsterdam C.S.-Hoorn/Amersfoort and Utrecht CS-Leiden/Baarn/Amsterdam CS.

Built 1969-70 by Werkspoor (441-461) and Talbot (462-483). "1962 stock". Automatic doors PA.
Formation: ABk-Bk (DMCsoL–DMSsoL)   *Seats: 24F 40S + 78 S*
Traction motors: Four Smit 118 kW (158hp)
Weight: 85 t   *Max speed: 140 km/h (87 mph)*
Length: 52.14 m (170'3")

441	450	459	468	476
442	451	460	469	477
443	452	461	470	478
444	453	462	471	479
445	454	463	472	480
446	455	464	473	481
447	456	465	474	482
448	457	466	475	483
449	458	467		

Plan M two car 1954-type emu no. 362 at Utrecht CS on 23rd March 1983.
[Gordon Lacy

Plan V two-car 1962-type emu no. 458 at Nijmegen on 24th March 1982.
[Gordon Lacy

PLAN TT   PROTOTYPE 4-CAR UNIT

Built: 1961 by Werkspoor. Prototype unit for 1962 stock. Automatic doors. PA.
Formation: Bk–AD–B–Bk (DTSsoL–MBFsoL– MSOL– DTSsoL)
Seats: 80S 1L +41F 1L +80S 1L
Traction motors: Eight Smit 175 kW (235hp)
Weight: 163 t   Max speed: 140 km/h (87 mph)
Length: 102 m (333'11½")
501

PLAN T   4-CAR UNITS

These sets operate over a more limited area, being normally confined to the
Dordrecht-Den Haag-Amsterdam C.S./Amsterdam RAI services, although they also
travel as far as Venlo on Den Haag stopping trains which are not covered by loco-hauled
sets.
Built: 1964-5 by Werkspoor. "1962 stock". Automatic doors. PA.
Formation: Bk–BD–AB–Bk (DTSsoL-MBSOL(K)–MCsoL–DTsoL)
Seats: 80S 1L + 24S 22 buffet 1L-42F 24S 1L-80S 1L
Traction motors: Eight Smit 175 kW (235hp)
Weight: 168 t   Max speed: 140 km/h (87 mph)
Length: 102 m (333'11½")

502	508	514	520	526
503	509	515	521	527
504	510	516	522	528
505	511	517	523	529
506	512	518	524	530
507	513	519	525	531

PLAN F,G&P   4-CAR UNITS

These four-car sets, which include a buffet, work indiscriminately with the refurbished
variety, principally on the services from Amsterdam and Den Haag/Rotterdam to
Groningen/Leeuwarden and Enschede. The Den Haag and Rotterdam services com-
bine at Utrecht C.S. and split again at Zwolle for their respective destinations and are
often strengthened, usually only as far as Zwolle, by a two-car (321 series) set. They
have largely been displaced from the Vlissingen to Amsterdam C.S. trains by loco-
hauled coaching sets as on the Den Haag C.S.-Venlo route, but often strengthen the
through Brussels-Amsterdam (see 1201 series) services from Roosendaal. They also
work some Amsterdam C.S.-Arnhem services and are still found on the Zwolle-
Roosendaal/Vlissingen route, usually covering for a missing loco and coaching stock
set.
Built by Werkspoor, Allan & Beijnes 1956-62. "1954 stock". Automatic doors. PA
Formation: Bk–A–B–BDK (DMSsoL–TFsoL–TSoL(K)-DMBSOL).
Seats: 72S 2L (plan F) 70S 2L (plan G/P) + 48F 1L + 56S 22 buffet 2L + 40S
Traction motors: Eight Smit-Heemaf 169 kW (227 hp)   Weight: 213 t (F,G) 206 t (P)
Max speed: 140 km/h (87 mph)
Length: 99.26 m (325'
711-741 were plan F, 742-757 plan G, 761-786 plan P. Many have been rebuilt and
renumbered in the 17xx series.

712	714	716	718	720
713	715	717	719	722

Plan T 1962-type 4-car emu no. 514 at Amsterdam Sloterdijk on 10th September 1981. [Gordon Lacy

Plan F 1954-type 4-car emu no. 719 at Groningen on 23rd March 1982. [Gordon Lacy

1600 Class Bo-Bo no. 1612 Goes at s'Hertogenbosh (23 March 1983). The front coach is a plan N-B10 (SK). [G.Lacy

New Plan Y3 "Sprinter" e.m.u. no 2890 at Amsterdam Centraal Station on 4th December 1983. [P. Fox

V.I.P. Single Car Unit no 20 at Amsterdam Centraal Station on 25th March 1982. This vehicle is known as "de Kameel" (the camel) on account of the two humps on its roof. [G.Lacy

Class DEI no 30 in red livery at Arnhem with the 11.01 to Teil on 9th September 1982. [G. Lacy

Postal Car no 3011 in New livery with 1100 class Bo-Bo no 1129 in the background at Den Haag H.S. on 26th March 1983. [G.Lacy

A pair of the new Utrecht-Nieuwegein "Sneltrams" (Fast trams) outside Utrecht C.S. on 4th December 1983, no. 5010 nearest. [P.Fox

2400 class Bo-Bo diesel electric no. 2490 in the old red livery heads an e.c.s. of "Eurofima" stock through Amsterdam Centraal station on 4th December 1982. [G.Lacy

Plan E open second no 50 84 29-37 324-6 at Breda on 4th December 1983. [P.Fox

723	728	739	752	770
724	730	740	753	771
725	734	742	754	772
726	736	747	756	774
727	738	751	769	

PLAN V   TWO-CAR UNITS

Built Werkspoor 1970-2 (801-40). For details see 441-483

801	809	817	825	833
802	810	818	826	834
803	811	819	827	835
804	812	820	828	836
805	813	821	829	837
806	814	822	830	838
807	815	823	831	839
808	816	824	832	840

PLAN V   TWO-CAR UNITS

841-965: These sets perform similar work to the 801 series, mainly to the South and West of the country on such routes as Amsterdam C.S.-Hoorn/Den Helder/Enkhuizen, Haarlem-Ijmuiden, Gouda-Alphen a/d Rijn, Maastricht-Heerlen/Sittard, etc.

Built: Talbot 1972-6. Similar to 801-840, but with post compartment.
Formation: ABk-BPk (DMCsoL–DMPSOL). Seats: 24F 40S 1L +56S 1L[1]
Traction motors: Four Smit 188 kW (252 hp) Weight: 86 t
Max speed: 140 km/h (87 mph) Length: 52.14 m (170'3")

841	866	892	917	941
842	867	893	918	942
843	868	894	919	943
844	869	895	920	944
845	870	896	921	945
846	871	897	922	946
847	872	898	923	947
848	873	899	924	948
849	874	900	925	949
850	875	901	926	950
851	876	902	927	951
852	877	903	928	952
853	879	904	929	953
854	880	905	930	954
855	881	906	931	955
856	882	907	932	956
857	883	908	933	957
858	884	909	934	958
859	885	910	935	960
860	886	911	936	961
861	887	912	937	962
862	888	913	938	963
863	889	914	939	964
864	890	915	940	965
865	891	916		

Benelux two car unit no. 1201 at Amsterdam C.S. on 24th March 1983. [Gordon Lacy

Refurbished plan G 4-car unit no. 1762 at Roosendaal on 11th September 1982.   [Gordon Lacy

BENELUX
2-CAR UNITS

These dual-current two-car sets generally work alternate services with the Benelux push-pull sets which are powered by S.N.C.B. 2551 series electric locomotives. The livery of dark blue, relieved by a yellow stripe, is also carried by the Belgian owned 220901-04 series with which these units interwork.

Built by Werkspoor "1954 stock"
Formation: ABk – BDk (DMCso–DMBSOL). The ABk carries 1500 V dc electrical equipment and the BDk 3000 V dc electrical equipment.
Seats: 24F 32S + 64S IL
Traction motors: Four ACEC 152 kW (204 hp)   *Weight: 116 t*
Max speed: 130 km×h (81 mph)   *Length: 51.12 m (167'4½")*
—Belgian units

1201	1204	1207	220901*	220903*
1202	1205	1208	220902*	220904*
1203	1206			

PLAN F-v, G-v & P-v
4-CAR UNITS

Rebuilt 1972-3 (1780-91) 1975-8 (others) with Inter-City (undirectional) second class seating. Livery changed to dark blue over windows with yellow below. 1780-91 also have undirectional seating in the first class saloon. Details as for 712-774 except:

Seats: 32S + 48S 22 buffet 2L + 48F 1L (45F 1L 1780-91) + 42S 2L

1780-91 have all over blue doors. 1000 has been added to the former numbers except where shown.

1711	1743	1757	1767	1785
1721	1744	1761	1768	1786
1729	1745	1762	1780	1787 (773)
1731	1746	1763	1781	1788 (775)
1733	1748	1764	1782	1789 (777)
1735	1749	1765	1783	1790 (778)
1737	1750	1766	1784	1791 (779)
1741	1755			

TREINSTEL 1970 (PLAN P-v)
4-CAR UNIT

Rebuilt 1970 as prototype for future. Details as for 712-774 except:
Formation: Ak—Ar—A—Bk. (DMFO—TFOLRB—FsoL—DMSsoL)
Seats: 45F+31F 22 buffet 2L + 48F 1L + 42S 1L. The buffet car first class seats are now declassified. The unit is usually to be found in the Rotterdam/Amsterdam-Amersfoort area.

1970 (776)

PLAN Y0-SPRINTER SGM0
2-CAR UNITS

The earliest batch of "Sprinter" units, these sets work on the Zoetermeer Stadslijn which is a circular route through the eastern suburbs of Den Haag, served from C.S. station. The rapid acceleration from a standing start is especially useful on this line which has stations at very close intervals.

Built: 1975-6 by Talbot. Non gangwayed. Automatic doors. Disc brakes. PA.
Formation: ABk-Bk (DMCO-DMSO)
Traction Motors: Eight Oerlikon 160 kW (215 hp)
Max speed: 125 km/h (77.5 mph)

Seats: 32F 40S +72S
Weight: 105 t
Length: 52.2 m (171'3")

2001	2004	2007	2010	2013
2002	2005	2008	2011	2014
2003	2006	2009	2012	2015

PLAN Y1-SPRINTER SGM1 2-CAR UNITS

Built 1978-80 by Talbot. Similar workings to Plan Y0. Automatic doors. Disc brakes. PA.
Formation: ABk-Bk (DMCO-DMSOL)
Traction motors: Eight Oerlikon 160 кW (215 hp)
Max speed: 125 km/h (77.5 mph)

Seats: 32F 40S +72S 1L
Weight: 106 t
Length: 52.3 m (171'7")

2021	2024	2027	2030	2033
2022	2025	2028	2031	2034
2023	2026	2029	2032	2035

PLAN Y2-SPRINTER SGM1 2 or 3-CAR UNITS

These two-car "Sprinter" units, most of which are being converted to three-car and renumbered in the 28xx series, are mainly confined to routes in the west of the country around Rotterdam and Den Haag and work such turns as Den Haag C.S.-Leiden-Amsterdam C.S., Den Haag C.S.-Rotterdam-Dordrecht-Roosendaal, Den Haag-Rotterdam Hofplein and Rotterdam C.S.-Hoek van Holland.

Details as for 2021-35. When converted to three car units the ABk (DMCO) is declassified and seats 72S (The "first class" seats were similar to the second class anyway). The new trailer is an AB(TCO) seating 40F 40S and taking the weight to 142 t and the length to 78.6 m (257'10").

2836 (2036)	2845 (2045)	2054	2863 (2063)	2072
2837 (2037)	2846 (2046)	2055	2064	2073
2838 (2038)	2847 (2047)	2056	2865 (2065)	2074
2839 (2039)	2848 (2048)	2857 (2057)	2066	2075
2840 (2040)	2849 (2049)	2058	2067	2076
2841 (2041)	2850 (2050)	2059	2068	2077
2842 (2042)	2051	2060	2869 (2069)	2878 (2078)
2843 (2043)	2852 (2052)	2861 (2061)	2070	2079
2844 (2044)	2053	2062	2871 (2071)	2880 (2080)

PLAN Y3-SPRINTER SGM2 3-CAR UNITS

Built 1983. Similar to 2836-80

2881	2884	2887	2890	2893
2882	2885	2888	2891	2894
2883	2886	2889	2892	2895

PLAN mP SINGLE UNIT POSTAL VANS

The postal units, which are painted in plain dark red or the new crimson/yellow livery, are unique amongst the N.S. units in having conventional drawgear and buffers to facilitate the taking of a trailing load of special postal vans. They can been seen stabled at most of the principal centres during the daytime as most of their workings occur during the night hours.

Built 1965-6 by Werkspoor.
Traction motors: Four Smit-Heemat 145 kW (194 hp)   Weight: 52 t
Max speed: 140 km/h (87 mph)   Length: 26.4 m (86'7'')
*—In new red/yellow livery

3001*	3008*	3016*	3024	3030
3002*	3009*	3017*	3025	3031
3003*	3011*	3018	3026	3032
3004	3012*	3019*	3027	3033
3005*	3013	3020	3028	3034
3006*	3014	3022	3029*	3035
3007	3015	3023		

DIESEL HYDRAULIC MULTIPLE UNITS

These new units represent a change in policy for the N.S. having hydraulic transmission. Their appearance is much more bus-like having flattened ends with one-piece windscreens. The 3201 series which have been introduced in the North and cover duties of all of the branch lines from Groningen having taken over from 61,111 and 161 series. Early problems with the disc brakes (similar to those of B.R.'s class 508 units) caused some temporary reversion to the original sets, but scrubber blocks have now been fitted.

3100 SERIES   SINGLE UNITS
Built 1983 by Duewag.
Engine: One Cummins NT 855 R4 of 212 kW (284 hp).
Transmission: Voith T211r   Length: 22.31 m (73'2'')
Formation: mB (DMSOL)   Seats: 56S 1L
Mx speed: 100 km/h (62.5 mph)   Weight: 36 t.

3101	3105	3109	3113	3117
3102	3106	3110	3114	3118
3103	3107	3111	3115	3119
3104	3108	3112	3116	

3200 SERIES   2-CAR UNITS
Built: 1981-2 by Duewag
Engine: One Cummins NT855R4 of 212 kW (284 hp) per car.
Transmission: Voith T211r   Length: 43.45 m (42'7'')
Formation: Bk–Bk (DMSOL-DMSO)   Seats: 68S 1L + 72S
Max speed: 100 km/h (62.5 mph)   Weight: 70 t

3201	3208	3214	3220	3226
3202	3209	3215	3221	3227
3203	3210	3216	3222	3228
3204	3211	3217	3223	3229
3205	3212	3218	3224	3230
3206	3213	3219	3225	3231
3207				

3200 class diesel hydraulic unit no. 3216 at Rodeschool.   [Allan Dare

Plan Z0 (IC3) unit no. 4003 leaving Amsterdam C.S. on 4th December 1983.
[Peter Fox

INTER-CITY ELECTRIC MULTIPLE UNITS

PLAN X0(IC3)   3-CAR UNITS

These striking modern units with their raised cabs and through corridor connections work solely on the Amsterdam C.S.-Utrecht-Arnhem-Nijmegen route, usually in pairs. The yellow/blue liveried coaches used in these sets formed the basis for the new-style loco-hauled stock now familiar over N.S. routes.

Built 1977 by Talbot. Automatic doors. Disc brakes. PA.
Formation: MBDk-AB-sBK (DMSO-TCOL (pantry)-DTSOL) Seats: 52S+35F31S+72S
Traction motors: Four Oerlikon 312.5kW (419 hp)   Weight: 142 t
Max speed: 160 km/h (100 mph)   Length: 80.6 m (264'5")

4001	4003	4005	4006	4007
4002	4004			

PLAN Z1 (IC3)   3-CAR UNITS

On order. Production version of IC3 units for delivery 1984 onwards.
Details as plan Z0 except:
Seats: 54S+35F 30S+68S

4011	4029	4047	4064	4081
4012	4030	4048	4065	4082
4013	4031	4049	4066	4083
4014	4032	4050	4067	4084
4015	4033	4051	4068	4085
4016	4034	4052	4069	4086
4017	4035	4053	4070	4087
4018	4036	4054	4071	4088
4019	4037	4055	4072	4089
4020	4038	4056	4073	4090
4021	4039	4057	4074	4091
4022	4040	4058	4075	4092
4023	4041	4059	4076	4093
4024	4042	4060	4077	4094
4025	4043	4061	4078	4095
4026	4044	4062	4079	4096
4027	4045	4063	4080	4097
4028	4046			

TRAMS

The new tramway from Utrecht to Nieuwegein is operated by the West Nederland Bus Company, but the vehicles are owned by the NS.

SNELTRAM UTRECHT-NIEUWEGEIN
6-AXLE ARTIC CARS

Built 1981-83 by SIG Neuhausen, Switzerland. 750 V dc overhead.
Traction motors: Two Brown Boveri 228 kW (306 hp)   Seats: 98
Max speed: 80 km/h (50 mph)   Length: 29.8 m (97'9").

5001	5007	5013	5018	5023
5002	5008	5014	5019	5024
5003	5009	5015	5020	5025
5004	5010	5016	5021	5026
5005	5011	5017	5022	5027
5006	5012			

LOCOMOTIVE HAULED COACHING STOCK

GENERAL

Locomotive-hauled coaching stock on the NS is generally referred to by its type or "Plan". At the head of each class will be found the NS designation at the left hand side, with the British type code at the right. The NS type code consists of the "Plan" plus the NS designation as described on page 3.

After A or B comes the number compartments (or windows in open stock) for each class type, e.g. A3 B5 — three first class and five second class compartments. This does not apply to the new ICR stock.

British type codes are as used in Coaching Stock Pocket Book (see page 3).

Four types of stock are in service:

(a) **Internal stock.** As its title suggests, this stock may only work on NS lines. Train heating is 1000 V 50 Hz and 1500 V dc only.

(b) **"Buurland" stock.** This stock may work into adjacent countries, i.e. West Germany and Belgium. Train heating—all voltages.

(c) **Benelux stock.** Special stock for the Amsterdam-Brussels service. Benelux stock operates on all eth voltages, except for the driving trailers which operate on 3000 V dc only.

(d) **International stock.** May work anywhere. Train heating—all voltages.

NUMBERING SYSTEM

NS loco-hauled coaches are numbered according to the UIC standard system. The number consists of four pairs of digits, which describe owner, speed, heating type etc., a three digit serial number and a check digit. The system is as follows.

(a) Digits 1 and 2 indicate the exchange condition.

- 50 Passenger coach — internal use only
- 51 Passenger coach — international use.
- 60 Departmental passenger coach
- 61 Special service hauled stock
- 71 Sleeping cars — international use.

(b) Digits 3 and 4. These give the Railway of origin, e.g:

- 80 Deutsche Bundesbahn (DB) — German Federal Railways.
- 84 Nederlandse Spoorwegen (NS)
- 87 SNCF (French Railways)
- 88 SNCB (Belgian Railways)

(c) Digits 5 and 6. The fifth digit gives the class or type of vehicle.

- 1 First class
- 2 Second class
- 3 Composite
- 4 Couchette—first class
- 5 Couchette—second class or composite
- 6 Sleeping car—first class
- 7 Sleeping car—second class or composite
- 8 Special purpose vehicle
- 9 Postal or Luggage van

The sixth digit gives the number of compartments (or windows/seating bays in the case of open stock).

- 0 10 compartments or bays
- 1 11 compartments or bays

2 12 compartments or bays
3 six-wheeled carriage
4 Four-wheeled carriage
5 Reserved
6 6 compartments or bays or double decker
7 7 compartments or bays
8 8 compartments or bays
9 9 compartments or bays
(d) Digit 7 and 8. These give the maximum speed and type of operation.*Digit 7*
0 120 km/h, electric heating
1 120 km/h, hual heating
2 120 km/h, steam heating (except for 26,27,28—Dual, 29—no heating)
3 121-140 km/h, electric heating
4/5 121-140 km/h, dual heating
6 121-140 km/h, steam heating (except for 69—no heating)
7 141-160 km/h electric heating
8 141-160 km/h dual heating (except 84—steam 89—no heating
9 Above 160 km/h

Digit 8 sometimes depends upon digit 7, but in general:
0 All voltages
6 All voltages except 3000 V dc
7 1500 V dc or 50 Hz ac
8 3000 V dc
9 If digit 8 is 0,1,7—3000 V dc. If digit 8 is 3,4,5—3,000 V dc + 1000 V $16\frac{2}{3}$ Hz ac.
digits 9,10 and 11. These give the serial number of the individual vehicle.

digit 12. This gives the check digit. Multiply as follows:

Digit	1 2	3 4	5 6	7 8 9 10 11
X	2 1	2 1	2 1	2 1 2 1 2

Add all resultant digits and subtract the last number of the result from 10. This gives the check digit, example:

	5 0	8 4	2 9	3 7	2 4 8
X	2 1	2 1	2 1	2 1	2 1 2

$1+0+0+1+6+4+4+9+6+7+4+4+1+6$ = 53

Subtract 3 from 10 — check digit is 7

DIESEL HAULED GENERATOR VANS
Built 1970-1 by Alsthom on goods wagon frames. These vans have two Alsthom 160 kW diesel generators. Four wheeled. Used with plan E stock for diesel hauled services. Out of use at time of writing.

21 84 95 42 501-7	21 84 95 42 504-1	21 84 95 42 506-6
21 84 95 42 502-5	21 84 95 42 505-8	21 84 95 42 507-4

PLAN ICR-A1   Fso
Built 1981 onwards by Talbot. "Buurland" stock. Pressure ventilated. Power operated plug doors. Disc braked pa 59 F 1L (35 F in saloon 24 Fin 4 compartments) 26.4 m long over buffers. 41 t.

50 84 10-70 651-1	50 84 10-70 655-2	50 84 10-70 661-0
50 84 10-70 652-9	50 84 10-70 656-0	50 84 10-70 662-8
50 84 10-70 653-7	50 84 10-70 657-8	50 84 10-70 663-6
50 84 10-70 654-5	50 84 10-70 658-6	50 84 10-70 664-4

50 84 10-70 665-1	50 84 10-70 674-3	50 84 10-70 682-6
50 84 10-70 666-9	50 84 10-70 675-0	50 84 10-70 683-4
50 84 10-70 667-7	50 84 10-70 676-8	50 84 10-70 684-2
50 84 10-70 668-5	50 84 10-70 677-6	50 84 10-70 685-9
50 84 10-70 671-9	50 84 10-70 678-4	50 84 10-70 686-7
50 84 10-70 672-7	50 84 10-70 681-8	50 84 10-70 687-5
50 84 10-70 673-5		

BENELUX REPLACEMENT STOCK
On order. Similar to ICR-A1

50 84 10-70 _01-_	50 84 10-70 _05-_	50 84 10-70 _08-_
50 84 10-70 _02-_	50 84 10-70 _06-_	50 84 10-70 _11-_
50 84 10-70 _03-_	50 84 10-70 _07-_	50 84 10-70 _12-_
50 84 10-70 _04-_		

PLAN ICR-A2   SEMI-OPEN FIRST (Fso)

Built 1982 onwards by Talbot. Internal stock. Pressure ventilated. Power operated plug doors. Disc braked. pa. 59FIL (35F in saloon 24F in 4 compartments) 26.4 m long over buffers. 41t.

50 84 10-77 601-9	50 84 10-77 614-2	50 84 10-77 627-4
50 84 10-77 602-7	50 84 10-77 615-9	50 84 10-77 628-2
50 84 10-77 603-5	50 84 10-77 616-7	50 84 10-77 631-6
50 84 10-77 604-3	50 84 10-77 617-5	50 84 10-77 632-4
50 84 10-77 605-0	50 84 10-77 618-3	50 84 10-77 633-2
50 84 10-77 606-8	50 84 10-77 621-7	50 84 10-77 634-0
50 84 10-77 607-6	50 84 10-77 622-5	50 84 10-77 635-7
50 84 10-77 608-4	50 84 10-77 623-3	50 84 10-77 636-5
50 84 10-77 611-8	50 84 10-77 624-1	50 84 10-77 637-3
50 84 10-77 612-6	50 84 10-77 625-8	50 84 10-77 638-1
50 84 10-77 613-4	50 84 10-77 626-6	

PLAN E-A8   SEMI-OPEN FIRST (Fso)

Built 1954-6 by Beijnes. Internal stock of low profile. Hand operated sliding doors. 48F 2L (12F in each of two open saloons and 24F in 4 compartments). 23.05 m long over buffers. 45t.

50 84 18-37 201-1	50 84 18-37 218-5	50 84 18-37 237-5
50 84 18-37 202-9	50 84 18-37 221-9	50 84 18-37 238-3
50 84 18-37 203-7	50 84 18-37 222-7	50 84 18-37 241-7
50 84 18-37 204-5	50 84 18-37 223-5	50 84 18-37 242-5
50 84 18-37 205-2	50 84 18-37 224-3	50 84 18-37 243-3
50 84 18-37 206-0	50 84 18-37 225-0	50 84 18-37 244-1
50 84 18-37 207-8	50 84 18-37 226-8	50 84 18-37 245-8
50 84 18-37 208-6	50 84 18-37 227-6	50 84 18-37 246-6
50 84 18-37 211-0	50 84 18-37 228-4	50 84 18-37 247-4
50 84 18-37 212-8	50 84 18-37 231-8	50 84 18-37 248-2
50 84 18-37 213-6	50 84 18-37 232-6	50 84 18-37 251-6
50 84 18-37 214-4	50 84 18-37 233-4	50 84 18-37 252-4
50 84 18-37 215-1	50 84 18-37 234-2	50 84 18-37 253-2
50 84 18-37 216-9	50 84 18-37 235-9	50 84 18-37 254-0
50 84 18-37 217-7	50 84 18-37 236-7	50 84 18-37 255-7

Plan E semi-open first no. 50 84 18-37 237-5 at Breda on 4th December 1983.
[Peter Fox

Plan ICR-B2 no. 50 84 20-77 758-5 at Amsterdam C.S. on 4th December 1983.
[Peter Fox

PLAN N-B10   CORRIDOR SECOND (SK)

Built 1958-9 by Werkspoor as couchettes for international trains and later converted into 2nd class carriages. Slam doors. 80S 2L 2W. 25.5 m long buffers. 44t.

50 84 20-37 002-7	50 84 20-37 008-4	50 84 20-37 021-7
50 84 20-37 003-5	50 84 20-37 014-2	50 84 20-37 023-3
50 84 20-37 006-8	50 84 20-37 015-9	50 84 20-37 031-6
50 84 20-37 007-6	50 84 20-37 016-7	

PLAN ICR-BI   OPEN SECOND (TSO)

Built 1980-81 by Talbot. "Buurland" stock. Pressure ventilated. Power operated plug doors. Disc brakes. 80S IL. 26.4 m over buffers. 40t.

50 84 20-70 801-0	50 84 20-70 825-9	50 84 20-70 851-5
50 84 20-70 802-8	50 84 20-70 826-7	50 84 20-70 852-3
50 84 20-70 803-6	50 84 20-70 827-5	50 84 20-70 853-1
50 84 20-70 804-4	50 84 20-70 828-3	50 84 20-70 854-9
50 84 20-70 805-1	50 84 20-70 831-7	50 84 20-70 855-6
50 84 20-70 806-9	50 84 20-70 832-5	50 84 20-70 856-4
50 84 20-70 807-7	50 84 20-70 833-3	50 84 20-70 857-2
50 84 20-70 808-5	50 84 20-70 834-1	50 84 20-70 858-0
50 84 20-70 811-9	50 84 20-70 835-8	50 84 20-70 861-4
50 84 20-70 812-7	50 84 20-70 836-6	50 84 20-70 862-2
50 84 20-70 813-5	50 84 20-70 837-4	50 84 20-70 863-0
50 84 20-70 814-3	50 84 20-70 838-2	50 84 20-70 864-8
50 84 20-70 815-0	50 84 20-70 841-6	50 84 20-70 865-5
50 84 20-70 816-8	50 84 20-70 842-4	50 84 20-70 866-3
50 84 20-70 817-6	50 84 20-70 843-2	50 84 20-70 867-1
50 84 20-70 818-4	50 84 20-70 844-0	50 84 20-70 868-9
50 84 20-70 821-8	50 84 20-70 845-7	50 84 20-70 871-3
50 84 20-70 822-6	50 84 20-70 846-5	50 84 20-70 872-1
50 84 20-70 823-4	50 84 20-70 847-3	50 84 20-70 873-9
50 84 20-70 824-2	50 84 20-70 848-1	50 84 20-70 874-7

BENELUX REPLACEMENT STOCK
OPEN SECOND (TSO)

On order. Similar to ICR-B1.

50 84 20-70 _01-_	50 84 20 70 _07-_	50 84 20 70 _15-_
50 84 20-70 _02-_	50 84 20 70 _08-_	50 84 20 70 _16-_
50 84 20-70 _03-_	50-84 20 70 _11-_	50 84 20 70 _17-_
50 84 20-70 _04-_	50 84 20 70 _12-_	50 84 20 70 _18-_
50 84 20-70 _05-_	50 84 20 70 _13-_	50 84 20 70 _21-_
50 84 20-70 _06-_	50 84 20 70 _14-_	50 84 20 70 _22-_

PLAN ICR-B2   OPEN SECOND (TSO)

Built 1982 by Talbot. Internal stock. Pressure ventilated. Power operated plug doors. Disc brakes. pa. 80S IL. 26.4 m over buffers. 40 t.

Plan W1 (Benelux) open second no. 50 84 21-30 462-9 Amsterdam C.S. on 4th December 1983. [Peter Fox

Plan W2 open second in new livery no. 50 84 21-37 502-5 at Arnhem on 4th December 1983. [Peter Fox

50 84 20-77 701-5	50 84 20-77 725-4	50 84 20-77 751-0
50 84 20-77 702-3	50 84 20-77 726-2	50 84 20-77 752-8
50 84 20-77 703-1	50 84 20-77 727-0	50 84 20-77 753-6
50 84 20-77 704-9	50 84 20-77 728-8	50 84 20-77 754-4
50 84 20-77 705-6	50 84 20-77 731-2	50 84 20-77 755-1
50 84 20-77 706-4	50 84 20-77 732-0	50 84 20-77 756-9
50 84 20-77 707-2	50 84 20-77 733-8	50 84 20-77 757-7
50 84 20-77 708-0	50 84 20-77 734-6	50 84 20-77 758-5
50 84 20-77 711-4	50 84 20-77 735-3	50 84 20-77 761-9
50 84 20-77 712-2	50 84 20-77 736-1	50 84 20-77 762-7
50 84 20-77 713-0	50 84 20-77 737-9	50 84 20-77 763-5
50 84 20-77 714-8	50 84 20-77 738-7	50 84 20-77 764-3
50 84 20-77 715-5	50 84 20-77 741-1	50 84 20-77 765-0
50 84 20-77 716-3	50 84 20-77 742-9	50 84 20-77 766-8
50 84 20-77 717-1	50 84 20-77 743-7	50 84 20-77 767-6
50 84 20-77 718-9	50 84 20-77 744-5	50 84 20-77 768-4
50 84 20-77 721-3	50 84 20-77 745-2	50 84 20-77 771-8
50 84 20-77 722-1	50 84 20-77 746-0	50 84 20-77 772-6
50 84 20-77 723-9	50 84 20-77 747-8	50 84 20-77 773-4
50 84 20-77 724-7	50 84 20-77 748-6	50 84 20-77 774-2

PLAN W1-B11 OPEN SECOND (TSO)

Built Werkspoor 1966-7. Benelux push and pull stock. Swivel doors. pa 88S IL. 26.4 m over buffers. 35t.

50 84 21-30 451-1	50 84 21-30 461-0	50 84 21-30 471-9
50 84 21-30 452-9	50 84 21-30 462-8	50 84 21-30 472-7
50 84 21-30 453-7	50 84 21-30 463-6	50 84 21-30 473-5
50 84 21-30 454-5	50 84 21-30 464-4	50 84 21-30 474-3
50 84 21-30 455-2	50 84 21-30 465-1	50 84 21-30 475-0
50 84 21-30 456-0	50 84 21-30 466-9	50 84 21-30 476-8
50 84 21-30 457-8	50 84 21-30 467-7	50 84 21-30 477-6
50 84 21-30 458-6	50 84 21-30 468-5	

PLAN W2-B11 OPEN SECOND (TSO)

Built Werkspoor 1968. Similar to Plan W1 but for internal use only. At present being refurbished and repainted in yellow and black livery. pa. 88SIL. 26.4 m over buffers. 35t.

50 84 21-37 501-7	50 84 21-37 513-2	50 84 21-37 523-1
50 84 21-37 502-5	50 84 21-37 514-0	50 84 21-37 524-9
50 84 21-37 503-3	50 84 21-37 515-7	50 84 21-37 525-6
50 84 21-37 505-8	50 84 21-37 516-5	50 84 21-37 526-4
50 84 21-37 506-6	50 84 21-37 517-3	50 84 21-37 527-2
50 84 21-37 507-4	50 84 21-37 518-1	50 84 21-37 528-0
50 84 21-37 508-2	50 84 21-37 521-5	50 84 21-37 531-4
50 84 21-37 511-6	50 84 21-37 522-3	50 84 21-37 532-2
50 84 21-37 512-4		

DOUBLE-DECK SECONDS

On order for Amsterdam-Den Helder service. Push and pull fitted. Similar to SNCF double-deck stock. 156 S2L (72 Upper-deck; 84 lower-deck).

50 84 26-77 _01-_	50 84 26-77 _15-_	50 84 26-77 _28-_
50 84 26-77 _02-_	50 84 26-77 _16-_	50 84 26-77 _31-_
50 84 26-77 _03-_	50 84 26-77 _17-_	50 84 26-77 _32-_
50 84 26-77 _04-_	50 84 26-77 _18-_	50 84 26-77 _33-_
50 84 26-77 _05-_	50 84 26-77 _21-_	50 84 26-77 _34-_
50 84 26-77 _06-_	50 84 26-77 _22-_	50 84 26-77 _35-_
50 84 26-77 _07-_	50 84 26-77 _23-_	50 84 26-77 _36-_
50 84 26-77 _08-_	50 84 26-77 _24-_	50 84 26-77 _37-_
50 84 26-77 _11-_	50 84 26-77 _25-_	50 84 26-77 _38-_
50 84 26-77 _12-_	50 84 26-77 _26-_	50 84 26-77 _41-_
50 84 26-77 _13-_	50 84 26-77 _27-_	50 84 26-77 _42-_
50 84 26-77 _14-_		

PLAN E-B9   OPEN SECOND (TSO)

Built 1954-6 by Werkspoor. Internal stock of low profile. Hand operated sliding doors. 72 S 2L. 23.05 m long over buffers. 45t.

50 84 29-37 201-6	50 84 29-37 245-3	50 84 29-37 291-7
50 84 29-37 202-4	50 84 29-37 246-1	50 84 29-37 292-5
50 84 29-37 203-2	50 84 29-37 247-9	50 84 29-37 293-3
50 84 29-37 204-0	50 84 29-37 248-7	50 84 29-37 294-1
50 84 29-37 206-5	50 84 29-37 252-9	50 84 29-37 295-8
50 84 29-37 208-1	50 84 29-37 253-7	50 84 29-37 296-6
50 84 29-37 212-3	50 84 29-37 255-2	50 84 29-37 297-4
50 84 29-37 213-1	50 84 29-37 256-0	50 84 29-37 298-2
50 84 29-37 214-9	50 84 29-37 257-8	50 84 29-37 302-6
50 84 29-37 216-4	50 84 29-37 258-6	50 84 29-37 303-4
50 84 29-37 217-2	50 84 29-37 261-0	50 84 29-37 304-2
50 84 29-37 218-0	50 84 29-37 262-8	50 84 29-37 305-9
50 84 29-37 221-4	50 84 29-37 263-6	50 84 29-37 306-7
50 84 29-37 222-2	50 84 29-37 264-4	50 84 29-37 307-5
50 84 29-37 226-3	50 84 29-37 266-9	50 84 29-37 308-3
50 84 29-37 227-1	50 84 29-37 267-7	50 84 29-37 313-3
50 84 29-37 231-3	50 84 29-37 268-5	50 84 29-37 314-1
50 84 29-37 232-1	50 84 29-37 271-9	50 84 29-37 315-8
50 84 29-37 234-7	50 84 29-37 272-7	50 84 29-37 317-4
50 84 29-37 235-4	50 84 29-37 273-5	50 84 29-37 318-2
50 84 29-37 236-2	50 84 29-37 277-6	50 84 29-37 321-6
50 84 29-37 237-0	50 84 29-37 278-4	50 84 29-37 322-4
50 84 29-37 238-8	50 84 29-37 281-8	50 84 29-37 323-2
50 84 29-37 241-2	50 84 29-37 282-6	50 84 29-37 324-0
50 84 29-37 242-0	50 84 29-37 283-4	50 84 29-37 331-5
50 84 29-37 243-8	50 84 29-37 287-5	50 84 29-37 334-9
50 84 29-37 244-6	50 84 29-37 288-3	50 84 29-37 338-0

PLAN E-B9-DE   OPEN SECOND (TSO)

As Plan E-B9, but converted for push and pull working with a 2200 class diesel at each end. At the time of writing these coaches are used on electric-hauled trains.

50 84 29-37 351-9	50 84 29-37 358-4	50 84 29-37 367-5
50 84 29-37 352-7	50 84 29-37 361-8	50 84 29-37 368-3
50 84 29-37 353-5	50 84 29-37 362-6	50 84 29-37 371-7
50 84 29-37 354-3	50 84 29-37 363-4	50 84 29-37 372-5
50 84 29-37 355-0	50 84 29-37 364-2	50 84 29-37 373-3
50 84 29-37 356-8	50 84 29-37 365-9	50 84 29-37 374-1
50 84 29-37 357-6	50 84 29-37 366-7	

BENELUX REPLACEMENT STOCK
SEMI -OPEN COMPOSITE (Cso)

On order. No details yet available.

50 84 30-77 _01-_	50 84 30-77 _05-_	50 84 30-77 _08-_
50 84 30-77 _02-_	50 84 30-77 _06-_	50 84 30-77 _11-_
50 84 30-77 _03-_	50 84 30-77 _07-_	50 84 30-77 _12-_
50 84 30-77 _04-_		

DOUBLE DECKER COMPOSITE

On order for Amsterdam – Den Helder service. Push and Pull fitted. Similar to SNCF double-deck stock. 64 F 76 S (36 F 28 S upper deck, 28 F 48 S lower deck).

50 84 36-77 _01-_	50 84 36-77 _13-_	50 84 36-77 _25-_
50 84 36-77 _02-_	50 84 36-77 _14-_	50 84 36-77 _26-_
50 84 36-77 _03-_	50 84 36-77 _15-_	50 84 36-77 _27-_
50 84 36-77 _04-_	50 84 36-77 _16-_	50 84 36-77 _28-_
50 84 36-77 _05-_	50 84 36-77 _17-_	50 84 36-77 _31-_
50 84 36-77 _06-_	50 84 36-77 _18-_	50 84 36-77 _32-_
50 84 36-77 _07-_	50 84 36-77 _21-_	50 84 36-77 _33-_
50 84 36-77 _08-_	50 84 36-77 _22-_	50 84 36-77 _34-_
50 84 36-77 _11-_	50 84 36-77 _23-_	50 84 36-77 _35-_
50 84 36-77 _12-_	50 84 36-77 _24-_	

PLAN K-A3B5   CORRIDOR COMPOSITE (CK)

Built 1957-8 by Beijnes. Slam doors. Certain of these coaches have been bought back from scrapyards or preservation societies. They will probably be resold to them in a few years time. Slam doors 18F 40S 2L 2W. 22.65 m long over buffers. 49 t. :

50 84 38-37 055-5	50 84 38-37 065-4	50 84 38-37 077-9
50 84 38-37 056-3	50 84 38-37 068-8	50 84 38-37 082-9
50 84 38-37 058-9	50 84 38-37 071-2	50 84 38-37 083-7
50 84 38-37 061 3	50 84 38-37 074-6	50 84 38-37 084-5
50 84 38-37 063-9	50 84 38-37 076-1	

PLAN E-A2B7-DE   OPEN COMPOSITE (CO)

Converted from plan E-B9 for push and pull working with a 2200 class diesel at each end. These coaches have one second class saloon which seated 16 replaced by uncomfortable reclining seats arranged as three rows 2+2. 12F 56S 2L. 23.05 m long over buffers. 45t.

50 84 39-37 351-5	50 84 39-37 355-6	50 84 39-37 361-4
50 84 39-37 352-3	50 84 39-37 356-4	50 84 39-37 362-2
50 84 39-37 353-1	50 84 39-37 357-2	50 84 39-37 363-0
50 84 39-37 354-9	50 84 39-37 358-0	

PLAN ICR-BKD KITCHEN BRAKE OPEN SECOND (BSO(k))

Built 1981-2 by Talbot. "Buurland" stock. These vehicles consist of a brake open second with a kitchen area from which a trolley refreshment service operates. Pressure ventilated. pt. 53S IL. 24.60 m long over buffers. 41 t.

50 84 82-70 901-3	50 84 82-70 918-7	50 84 82-70 936-9
50 84 82-70 902-1	50 84 82-70 921-1	50 84 82-70 937-7
50 84 82-70 903-9	50 84 82-70 922-9	50 84 82-70 938-5
50 84 82-70 904-7	50 84 82-70 923-7	50 84 82-70 941-9
50 84 82-70 905-4	50 84 82-70 924-5	50 84 82-70 942-7
50 84 82-70 906-2	50 84 82-70 925-2	50 84 82-70 943-5
50 84 82-70 907-0	50 84 82-70 926-0	50 84 82-70 944-3
50 84 82-70 908-8	50 84 82-70 927-8	50 84 82-70 945-0
50 84 82-70 911-2	50 84 82-70 928-6	50 84 82-70 946-8
50 84 82-70 912-0	50 84 82-70 931-0	50 84 82-70 947-6
50 84 82-70 913-8	50 84 82-70 932-8	50 84 82-70 948-4
50 84 82-70 914-6	50 84 82-70 933-6	50 84 82-70 951-8
50 84 82-70 915-3	50 84 82-70 934-4	50 84 82-70 952-6
50 84 82-70 916-1	50 84 82-70 935-1	50 84 82-70 953-4
50 84 82-70 917-9		

BENELUX REPLACEMENT STOCK-BKD

On order. Probably similar to KR-BKD.

50 84 82-77 _01-_	50 84 82-77 _05-_	50 84 82-77 _08-_
50 84 82-77 _02-_	50 84 82-77 _06-_	50 84 82-77 _11-_
50 84 82-77 _03-_	50 84 82-77 _07-_	50 84 82-77 _12-_
50 84 82-77 _04-_		

DOUBLE DECKER DRIVING OPEN SECOND

On order from Talbot for Amsterdam-Den Helder service. Push and pull fitted. Similar to SNCF double-deck stock. 116 S (725 upper-deck, 44 lower-deck).

50 84 86-77 _01-_	50 84 86-77 _05-_	50 84 86-77 _11-_
50 84 86-77 _02-_	50 84 86-77 _06-_	50 84 86-77 _12-_
50 84 86-77 _03-_	50 84 86-77 _07-_	50 84 86-77 _13-_
50 84 86-77 _04-_	50 84 86-77 _08-_	50 84 86-77 _14-_

Plan E-Brake restaurant 50 84 87-37 216-3 at Breda on 4th December 1983.
[Peter Fox

One of the type WR (former "Apfelpfeil") restaurant cars at Amsterdam C.S. on 5th December 1983. (No. 51 84 88-40 014-5) [Peter Fox

PLAN E-rD   BRAKE RESTAURANT CAR (BRU)

Built 1955-6 by Beijnes. Internal stock of low profile. Hand operated sliding doors.
Consist of luggage and guards accommodation, kitchen and 22 seats. 23.05 m long over
buffers. 46 t.

50 84 87-37 201-5	50 84 87-37 212-2	50 84 87-37 223-9
50 84 87-37 202-3	50 84 87-37 213-0	50 84 87-37 224-7
50 84 87-37 203-1	50 84 87-37 214-8	50 84 87-37 225-4
50 84 87-37 204-9	50 84 87-37 215-5	50 84 87-37 226-2
50 84 87-37 205-6	50 84 87-37 216-3	50 84 87-37 227-0
50 84 87-37 206-4	50 84 87-37 217-1	50 84 87-37 228-8
50 84 87-37 207-2	50 84 87-37 218-9	50 84 87-37 231-2
50 84 87-37 208-0	50 84 87-37 221-3	50 84 87-37 232-0
50 84 87-37 211-4	50 84 87-37 222-1	

PLAN L-DF   BICYCLE BRAKE

Built 1958 by Werkspoor as post office vehicles. Converted 1983 to carry 30 bicycles
each. 23.05 m long over buffers. 45 t.

50 84 92-37 001-2	50 84 92-37 003-8	50 84 92-37 004-6
50 84 92-37 002-0		

TYPE SR   BUFFET & DANCING CAR (RB-SD)

Built 1953-4. International stock. Used on holiday trains and motorails. 26.4 m over
buffers. 42 t.

51 84 88-40 001-2	51 84 88-40 004-6	51 84 88-40 006-1
51 84 88-40 002-0	51 84 88-40 005-3	51 84 88-40 007-9
51 84 88-40 003-8		

TYPE WR   RESTAURANT CAR (RU)

Built 1954-5. International stock. Built originally for DB but recently owned by "Apfelpfeil" for holiday traffic. Bought by NS when Apfelpfeil went bankrupt in 1980. 26.4 m
long over buffers. Seats: 30 U. 42 t.

51 84 88-40 011-1	51 84 88-40 013-7	51 84 88-40 014-5
51 84 88-40 012-9		

PLAN D WRDk BENELUX DRIVING TRAILER (DRBU)

Built 1951 by Beijnes as WRD (BRU). Rebuilt by NS 1973-4 as push and pull driving
coaches for the Benelux service with the cab on the roof. Hand operated sliding doors.
Consists of driving cab, luggage and guards accommodation, 23 seats, a pantry and a
kitchen.

61 84 87-38 101-3	61 84 87-38 104-7	61 84 87-38 107-0
61 84 87-38 102-1	61 84 87-38 105-4	61 84 87-38 108-8
61 84 87-38 103-9	61 84 87-38 106-2	

The Royal Saloon built for Queen Juliana no. 61 84 89-40 001-9 prior to repainting on 5th December 1983. [Peter Fox

Plan D —Benelux driving trailer no. 61 84 87-38 104-7 heads an Amsterdam-Brussels train at Amsterdam C.S. on 5th December 1983. [Peter Fox

BENELUX REPLACEMENT DRIVING TRAILERS

On order. No details yet available.

61 84 87-78 _01-_   61 84 87-78 _05-_   61 84 87-78 _11-_
61 84 87-78 _02-_   61 84 87-78 _06-_   61 84 87-78 _12-_
61 84 87-78 _03-_   61 84 87-78 _07-_   61 84 87-78 _13-_
61 84 87-78 _04-_. 61 84 87-78 _08-_

ROYAL SALOONS

Built by Werkspoor in 1932 as composites. Rebuilt as Royal Saloons 1955/3 ...001 (formerly NS 9) was built for Queen Juliana and consists of a toilet, bathroom, bedroom, full width lounge, coupe, kitchen and attendants compartment with boiler, ...002 formerly (NS 8) was built for Prince Bernhard and Princess Beatrix and consists of two bedrooms, two bathrooms, a combined sitting and bedroom, an attendants compartments with boiler and a governess compartment. Weights: 56 t, 53 t. 21.8 m long over buffers.

61 84 89-40 001-9   61 84 89-40 002-7

SLEEPING CAR TYPE Mü   SLC

Built 1973 by Fiat. Sleeps up to 36. 28.4 m long over buffers. 55 t.
71 84 72-80 622-0

SLEEPING CAR TYPE T2S   SLSTP

Built 1975. 17 twin berth compartments. 26.4 m long over buffers. 55 t.
71 84 75-70 458-8   71 84 75-70 459-6

The 1000 class are now all withdrawn, although 1010 is preserved by "STIBANS". Here 1004 hauls a rake of plan N corridor seconds on an enthusiasts' railtour.[Mike Jacob

47

Plan K composite no. 50 84 38-37 084-5 at Amsterdam Centraal C.S. on 5th December 1983.   [Peter Fox

Plan ICR-BKD no. 50 84 82-70 905-4 at Amsterdam C.S. on 23rd March 1982. Note the folding steps which are a characteristic of "Buurland" stock compared with the rigid steps of internal stock. (c.f. page 37 bottom)   [Gordon Lacy

48